A GIFT FOR

Jenessa

❖ FROM ❖

Love Erin

Have Another Cookie
(It'll Make You Feel Better)

by
SCHULZ

Hallmark
BOOKS

HarperCollins*Publishers*

BOK 3003

Happiness
Is Only A Cookie
Away

Happiness Is Only A Cookie Away

SEE HOW MY HANDS SHAKE, CHARLES? IT'S BECAUSE OF ALL THE PRESSURE...

MY PARENTS THINK I SHOULD GET PERFECT GRADES IN EVERYTHING EVERY DAY!

One Is Never Enough

YOU SHOULD NEVER
EAT WITHOUT WARMING
UP FIRST!

HAT'S WHAT'S CALLED
PSETTING THE BALANCE
OF NATURE..

Doggie Bags
And
Cookies-To-Go

Doggie Bags And Cookies-To-Go

HEY,
PARTNER..

HOW DO YOU EXPECT
TO PLAY TENNIS AND
EAT COOKIES AT
THE SAME TIME?!

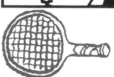

I CAN HANDLE THAT...

THE HARD PART IS RECEIVING SERVE WHILE DUNKING A COOKIE IN A GLASS OF MILK...

Doggie Bags And Cookies-To-Go

CHOCOLATE CHIP COOKIES
FOLLOW ME WHEREVER
I GO...

First published 1996 by Collins Publishers
Published under license from HarperCollins Publishers Inc.
Conceived and produced by Packaged Goods Incorporated
276 Fifth Avenue, New York, NY 10001
A Quarto Company

The Library of Congress has cataloged the original edition of this title as follows:
Schulz, Charles M.
(Peanuts. Selections)
Have another cookie / by Charles. Schulz.
p. cm.
"A Packaged Goods Incorporated Book"—T.P. verso
ISBN 0-00-225183-3
1. Title

PN6728.P483117   1996
741.5'973—dc 20   96-19378
                                                    CIP

ISBN 0-06-095395-0 (Hallmark edition)

01 02 03 RRD 10 9 8